SERIES 205

In this book, we will look at summer storms, carnivals, harvests and the solstice, as we explore the beauty of the summer.

LADYBIRD BOOKS

UK | USA | Canada | Ireland | Australia
India | New Zealand | South Africa

Ladybird Books is part of the Penguin Random House group of companies whose addresses can be found at global.penguinrandomhouse.com.

www.penguin.co.uk   www.puffin.co.uk   www.ladybird.co.uk

Penguin
Random House
UK

First published 2020
001

Copyright © Ladybird Books Ltd, 2020

Printed in Italy

A CIP catalogue record for this book is available from the British Library
ISBN: 978-0-241-41620-4

All correspondence to:
Ladybird Books
Penguin Random House Children's
One Embassy Gardens, New Union Square
5 Nine Elms Lane, London SW8 5DA

What to Look For in **Summer**

A Ladybird Book

Written by Elizabeth Jenner

Illustrated by Natasha Durley

Roe deer

These small, elegant deer with rusty-red summer coats are native to the British Isles, and have lived here for over 10,000 years. In seventeenth-century England, they were hunted to extinction, but were then reintroduced to the wild in the nineteenth century. The species thrived, and roe deer can now be seen in woodlands and forests all over Britain once more.

For the roe deer, summer is breeding season, otherwise known as "the rut". The male deer – called "bucks" – fight with each other aggressively for the attention of a female, or "doe". The winning buck then chases the doe for some time, until she decides she is ready to mate.

Although mating happens in the summer, the baby, or "kid", will not start to grow inside the doe until January. This means that the kids will be born in the late spring, when it is warmer. They then spend their days sitting in the long summer grasses while their mother watches over them.

Baby roe deer are born with spotted coats to camouflage them in the grass and protect them from predators. In a few months, when the kids are bigger and stronger, their spots will disappear. They will grow grey-brown coats, just like the adult deer, in time for the winter.

Busy bees

Summer is a busy time for bees. The long, warm days provide the perfect conditions for the worker honeybees to go out and collect nectar from flowers. The worker bees then take the nectar back to their hives.

Back at the hive, the bees drop the nectar they have collected into the honeycomb – a network of six-sided cells made from natural wax. Honeybees make their hexagonal honeycomb by eating honey. Their body changes the sugar content of the honey into wax, which oozes from their skin and flakes off. Worker bees chew the wax until it becomes soft enough to mould into cells.

When the nectar is first added to the honeycomb, it is very watery. In the heat of the hive, the water gradually evaporates, and the nectar becomes denser and stickier. The bees help this process by fanning the nectar with their wings. When the nectar has become a thick honey, the bees cover each honeycomb cell with a lid of wax, to store the honey safely. A beekeeper knows it is time to harvest the honey when they see a large area of sealed cells in a hive.

1. Garden bumblebee
2. "Ballad" sunflower
3. "Imperial gem" lavender
4. Human-made WBC beehive
5. "Serotina" honeysuckle
6. Honeybee
7. Honeycomb

1

2

3

4

5

6

7

Water voles

Down by the canal, the water voles come out of their burrows to nibble on the rushes. These small furry mammals like to live by waterways and ponds, eating mainly reeds and grasses. If you see small piles of chewed stems by the water's edge, you have found a water-vole restaurant!

Water voles are semi-aquatic, which means they live both on the land and in the water. Their burrows often have two entrances – one above ground, and one underwater – so that they can easily escape predators. They have little flaps of skin that cover their ears while they are swimming, to keep the water out.

A few years ago, there were hardly any water voles left in the British Isles. Their natural habitats were disappearing, and their numbers were threatened by the introduction of a new predator – the non-native American mink. A lot of conservation work is now being done to reintroduce water voles to our waterways and to make sure they stay there.

It's not just conservationists who are helping the water voles. Native river otters, which were also recently reintroduced, are rivals of the American mink. The otters' growing numbers mean that the mink now has fewer places to live and hunt.

Midsummer's Day

The longest day of the year falls at the end of June. This is the summer solstice – the day when the northern half of the earth is tilted furthest towards the sun, resulting in the year's longest period of daylight. The weather is warm, and plants, animals and humans all make the most of the extra light.

Briar roses and elderflowers bloom at this time of year. In this meadow, the grassland plants have produced seeds, so the farmer can harvest the grass. They will cut and dry the long stems to make hay, which will be used as feed for the farm animals. Swallows swoop through the sky during the long summer evenings, snapping up a few final insects before retiring to their nests for the night.

Midsummer has traditionally been marked in many ways, and is a celebration of fertility and hope for a good harvest. Some people celebrate on Midsummer's Eve with bonfires and feasts. Some go to church services or ancient religious sites. In England, thousands of people gather every year at the circle of standing stones at Stonehenge in Wiltshire, to acknowledge the summer solstice and watch the sun rise.

Strawberry picking

In summer, bright red strawberries start to peek out from under the leaves of these plants. After flowering early in the season, strawberry plants begin to produce fruit. The growing fruits start off small and green, and then ripen in the summer sunshine into big, red berries studded with seeds. The strawberries are then ready to be picked and eaten.

It's not just humans who like strawberries. These rabbits also have their eyes on this tasty snack! On this farm, the farmer has decided to grow the plants away from the ground, to prevent animals from eating all of the crop. However, blackbirds and other summer birds are also keen to help out with the picking, so it seems that the farmer can't protect the crop either way!

After the fruit has been picked, the strawberry plants put all of their energy into forming new flower buds before the colder weather returns. The buds will stay on the plant all through the winter, waiting for summer to return before they open and bloom.

Mackerel migration

These fish, with their shiny, tiger-like markings, are a common sight in the waters around the United Kingdom in summertime. The warmer weather brings them to shallow inshore waters, where they feed on small fish and plankton.

The mackerel's arrival is welcomed by fishers and also by other marine life. Atlantic mackerel are an important source of food for sharks, seals and dolphins, as well as many seabirds, such as the diving gannet.

The Atlantic mackerel is one of the fastest fish in the United Kingdom, as they are able to swim 50 metres (164 ft) in 10 seconds. They are powerful hunters, moving together in dense shoals like the one you see here. In big shoals, smaller fish trying to escape can be forced up to the surface of the water, making it look as though the sea is boiling!

Mackerel shoals spend the winter in deeper water, so they migrate away from the United Kingdom in the autumn. Some swim north-east towards the cold waters of Norway, then return to the shore in spring to spawn. However, mackerel in the west will go south to warmer waters, where they will spend the winter and then spawn before returning.

Bats at dusk

On warm summer evenings, look for bats flitting through the sky. Common pipistrelle bats are tempted out by all the moths and gnats that fly about at this time of day. A single pipistrelle can eat 3,000 gnats in one night!

Tiny pipistrelles are common throughout the United Kingdom. Like other bats, they are nocturnal – they come out to feed at dusk, before returning to their roosts at dawn, where they sleep during the day. In order to find their prey in the dark, they emit high-pitched squeaks, which bounce off the objects around them, allowing them to "see" their prey through sound. This is called "echolocation".

There are eighteen different species of bat in the United Kingdom. However, bat populations are in decline, as their natural habitats – especially trees and woodland – are being lost to human development.

Bats do not like to be disturbed, so any disruption to their habitat can have serious consequences. Every species of bat in the United Kingdom is now protected by law. This means that if you find bats roosting or hibernating on your property, it is illegal to disturb or remove them.

1. Brown long-eared bat
2. Buff-tip moth
3. Gnat
4. Lacewing
5. Common pipistrelle bat
6. Common mayfly
7. Eyed hawk-moth

1

2

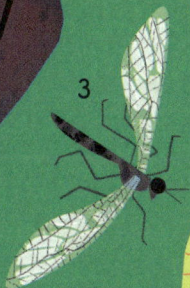

3

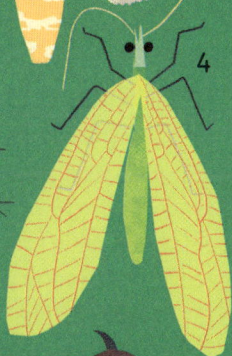

4

5

6

7

Dolphins in Cardigan Bay

If you go on holiday to Cardigan Bay in Wales, you are likely to meet one of the bay's most famous visitors – the biggest group, or "pod", of bottlenose dolphins within British waters. During the summer, the dolphins can be seen almost every day, swimming, playing and chasing fish.

The dolphins are attracted by the large number of fish in the bay, including bass, mullet, mackerel and salmon. The bay's wide variety of food makes it the perfect place for the dolphins to spend the summer and raise their young.

Bottlenose dolphins are marine mammals that live underwater, but they must come up to the surface to breathe. Unlike humans, who breathe using their mouth or nose, dolphins use a blowhole, which sits on the top of their head. They breathe in air when they rise above the water's surface, which they can then hold for up to seven minutes underwater.

Harbour porpoises, which are also marine mammals, live in the bay, too. You can tell porpoises and dolphins apart by their size and the shape of their dorsal fins. Dolphins tend to be much bigger and have a curved dorsal fin, whereas porpoises are smaller with a little triangular fin.

Keeping cool

It is a hot day in the city. The country is experiencing a heatwave – a period of time where temperatures rise to high levels. Heatwaves can happen in the United Kingdom during the summer, when weather patterns and higher levels of air pressure create long, dry spells.

Schools have broken up for the summer holidays, so everyone is out enjoying the sunshine. People sit in their gardens or find spots in the parks to have picnics. Families who live in cities might come to a city park to have fun and keep cool. Children paddle and play in the water, while pigeons take advantage of the extra crumbs that have been dropped on the paving stones.

As the sunlight dances through the fountains, a rainbow of sorts is created in the water. Rainbows appear when rays of light from the sun hit water droplets, which then reflect the light. Light travels more slowly through water than it does through air, so it bends as it passes through each raindrop. This makes the light split into a spectrum of different colours, which is called "refraction".

Flying Ant Day

Every year during the summer – usually in July, but on no fixed date – millions of ants take to the skies at the same time. This happens all over the United Kingdom and is known as Flying Ant Day. It is a time, usually lasting just one day, when male and young female ants sprout wings and leave their nests to seek out ants from other colonies to mate with. This is known as the "nuptial flight".

Most species of ant have a form of nuptial flight, but the most common type of ant seen on Flying Ant Day is the black garden, or "common black", ant. The female ants – called "queens" – will mate in flight with the males. They then land and try to start a new nest. If you see a big ant walking around after Flying Ant Day, it is probably a new queen looking for a place to make her nest.

Although Flying Ant Day can seem like a nuisance to humans, it is good news for birds and bats. Flying ants are a great source of food, and the birds and bats will make the most of this feast.

1. Winged black garden ant
2. Eggs
3. Black garden ant
4. Larvae of black garden ant
5. Winged black garden ant

Summer hunting

An osprey circles high above a Scottish lake, or "loch", looking for a rainbow trout in the water. It spots its prey, and hovers above the fish, waiting for just the right moment . . .

It dives towards the water, sharp and swift as an arrow, folding in its wings. At the last moment, it whips its feet out in front of its body, and uses its powerful talons to capture the wriggling fish.

Ospreys are birds of prey and they mostly eat fish. They have incredible talons that are specially adapted for catching their food. On each foot, an osprey has three extremely long and sharp talons. It also has special scales on its toes to help it hold on to slippery fish. One of the talons on each foot is reversible – it can point backwards as well as forwards. This gives the osprey an even more powerful grip.

These birds also have incredible eyesight – it is said to be up to five times better than a human's. This allows them to see fish swimming under the water from a great distance, so they know exactly where and when to strike.

St Swithin's Day

St Swithin's Day is on 15 July, and it is a day that commemorates the ninth-century Bishop of Winchester who requested that, when he died, he be buried outside Winchester Cathedral, so that the rain would fall on him. However, his body was later moved inside the cathedral, and a great storm followed. People believed that the storm was caused by his anger. To this day, it is still said that if it rains on St Swithin's Day, it will carry on raining for 40 days, but if it stays dry, it will be a long, sunny summer!

These house martins are ready for either possibility. House martins build their nests using mud, and they position them on the outside walls of houses, under the eaves of the roof. The eaves help to protect the nests from both summer showers and the hot sun. Pairs of male and female house martins build their nests together, carrying mud and twigs from nearby streams and ponds in their beaks. When the nest is finished, the female will lay four or five white eggs in it.

House martins leave their nests and migrate to parts of Africa for the winter, where it is much warmer. However, when they return the next summer, the birds will often go back to the same nest.

"Blood moon"

These two people are looking up at the "blood moon".
This is caused by a lunar eclipse, which happens when the
earth passes between the moon and the sun, and the moon
is cast into shadow. A lunar eclipse is different from a solar
eclipse. During a solar eclipse, the moon passes between the
earth and the sun, which blocks out the sun's light and
makes it look dark. By contrast, during a lunar eclipse the
moon does not look dark, but instead turns red. As such,
this phenomenon is known as the "blood moon".

The moon looks red because the light from the sun is
scattered through the earth's atmosphere. Some of the light
bounces around to hit the moon, but blue light particles
scatter more easily than red light particles, which means that
more red light reaches the moon. This is why the moon
looks red.

Lunar eclipses are rarer than solar eclipses, and only a
maximum of three occur each year. If you are lucky enough
to see one, it's best to view it in a dark place in the
countryside, away from streetlights and houses, just like this
pair of campers.

In the cornfields

In late summer, farmers begin to pick the wheat in their fields, as the stalks are starting to bow with the weight of the ripening ears of grain. The sparrows have also noticed this, and they have come to the fields to feed. Soon the farmer will fire up the combine harvester to cut the wheat stalks and extract the grain, so the sparrows must make the most of the food while they can.

The long days and extra sunlight help crops like wheat to grow. Other plants, such as the red field poppy, yellow ragwort and creeping thistle, also thrive in the dry conditions and attract butterflies to feed on the nectar in their flowers.

Many different types of butterfly are about at this time of year. The warm conditions are good for them, both for feeding and for laying their eggs on plants. A lot of butterflies are easy to identify, as their names reflect their appearance. See if you can spot the common blue, the red admiral and the small tortoiseshell butterflies here.

1. Field poppy
2. Red admiral butterfly
3. Common wheat
4. House sparrow
5. Creeping thistle
6. Common blue butterfly
7. Small tortoiseshell butterfly
8. Meadow brown butterfly
9. Common ragwort

Sand and shore

It's fun to go to the beach on a warm August day. Lots of families head to the coast for their summer holidays, and spend their days playing in the sea and on the sand. The coastal birds enjoy the opportunity to sneak snacks from unguarded fish-and-chip wrappers and picnics.

There's lots to do by the shore. Some people like to relax and read. Others like to swim or surf on the waves in the sea. Children build sandcastles at the water's edge, and wait for the tide to come in and fill the moat with seawater.

The level of the sea rises and falls with the tides, which are caused by the gravitational pulls of the sun and the moon. As the moon rotates round the earth and the position of the sun changes, the level of water in the sea also changes, as it is pulled first in one direction and then the other. During low tide, the water is far away from the shore. At high tide, the water comes right up to the rocks.

At low tide, rock pools may be uncovered, allowing you to peek into the lives of the sea creatures that live there. Look for sand-coloured fish such as butterfish or blenny, the pink tentacles of a sea anemone, and small translucent prawns.

1. Beadlet anemone
2. Lesser black-backed gull
3. Bladder wrack seaweed
4. Serrated wrack seaweed
5. Shore crab
6. Butterfish
7. Common prawn

1
2
3

4
5

6
7

Wildflowers everywhere

There are not many areas of wild land left in the United Kingdom, due to modern methods of farming, so the lowland meadows that remain are rare and special.

In the summer, lowland meadows come alive with a riot of colourful flowers. Plants thrive in these wild conditions due to the damp soil found there. Look for stately yellow meadow buttercups, pretty pink cuckooflowers, starry golden marsh marigolds and the red egg-shaped heads of great burnet. The grass itself is called "crested dog's-tail", because its tufts look exactly like the wagging tail of a dog!

These meadows also support many different species of insect, which rely on the flowers and plants to live and breed. Large striped bumblebees buzz from flower to flower, feeding on the nectar. Rare blue southern damselflies bask on the leaves, and meadow grasshoppers nibble on the grasses.

Be sure to listen for the chirruping of the male grasshoppers. They rub their back legs against their wings to make a noise and attract females. After mating, the female grasshopper will lay her eggs in a pod in the soil, ready to hatch the following spring.

1. Crested dog's-tail
2. Common sorrel
3. Meadow buttercup
4. Southern damselfly
5. Meadow grasshopper
6. "Red thunder" great burnet
7. Cuckooflower
8. Marsh-marigold
9. White-tailed bumblebee

1

2

3

4

5

6

7

8

9

Summer heat

As the summer goes on, the hot weather begins to take its toll on the gardens. Days of high temperatures, scorching sunlight and little rain are not good for many plants.

Gardeners spend a lot of time watering their plants in the summer, to help keep them alive. However, it is not always possible to give them enough water, as there are often water shortages in the summer that stop people from using their garden hosepipes and sprinklers.

The grass on this lawn has become burnt and yellow in the sun, because it has not had enough water. Luckily, grass is a tough plant. It should recover and grow new green shoots once the cooler, wetter days of autumn arrive.

The sparrows and blue tits in the garden can also struggle in the heat. Unlike humans, birds don't sweat, and this means that they must find other ways to avoid overheating. They need clean water to drink, but it's just as important that they have somewhere to bathe, so they can cool down. You can help by making sure birdbaths are always filled, and by putting out extra bowls of water during hot days.

Summer storms

It is the end of another hot, unsettled day. Dark purple clouds gather in the sky, and spots of rain start to fall. Far away, there is a warning rumble of thunder, and then a lightning flash. A summer storm is coming.

Thunderstorms develop when the air is unstable. This is caused when a layer of warm air sits under a layer of cold air. As the sun heats up the air nearer to the ground, it starts to rise through the colder air, creating instability and lots of water droplets.

Tall clouds, known as "cumulonimbus" clouds, start to form, and the water droplets are carried high into the clouds, creating ice particles. As these ice particles bump against each other, they become charged with electric energy – some particles become positively charged and others become negative. The negative particles in the clouds become attracted to the positively charged ground below, creating a connection and a flash of light called "lightning". The rumble of thunder is caused when the air inside the cloud heats up as a result of the lightning flash.

Storms are more common in summer, because there is more warmth and energy from the sun available to create these conditions.

Adders on the moors

As the end of summer approaches, delicate pink and purple flowers start to appear on the North York Moors. The ling heather is blossoming. This plant lives on moorland, heathland and bogs, and its tough, woody stems grow close together, which gives it a bush-like appearance. Ling heather will flower into the autumn, providing nectar for the last of the summer's insects before the colder weather arrives.

The heather also offers a sheltered spot for this adder. Adders are the United Kingdom's only venomous snakes, but adder bites are very rare. They are shy creatures, and they prefer to slide away into the undergrowth when they see a human rather than attack. Adders eat mice, lizards and small birds. Their venom is injected with a bite from their fangs and paralyses their prey so that they can swallow it whole.

Adders can grow up to 80 centimetres (31 in.) in length. They have skins made of tough scales, but as the adder gets bigger it outgrows its skin and wriggles out of it to grow a new one! If you are lucky, you might find an old skin on the ground that an adder has left behind. The adder you see here has brown scales, but they can also be grey and black. The dark patterns on its back help to camouflage it among the moorland plants.

1. Ling heather
2. Short-eared owl
3. Wood mouse
4. Red grouse
5. Adder

1

2

3

5

4

A Ladybird Book

collectable books for curious kids

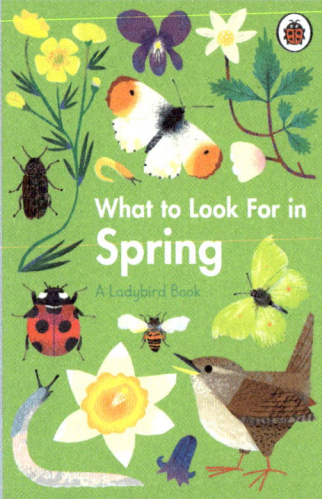

What to Look For in **Spring**

A Ladybird Book

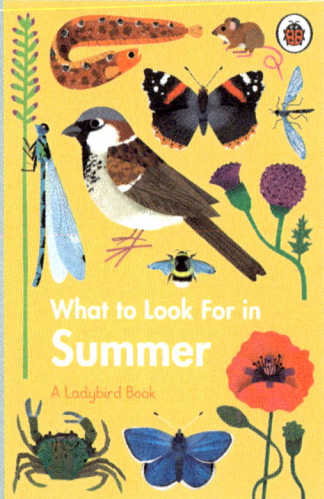

What to Look For in **Summer**

A Ladybird Book

What to Look For in Spring

9780241416181

What to Look For in Summer

9780241416204

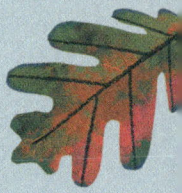

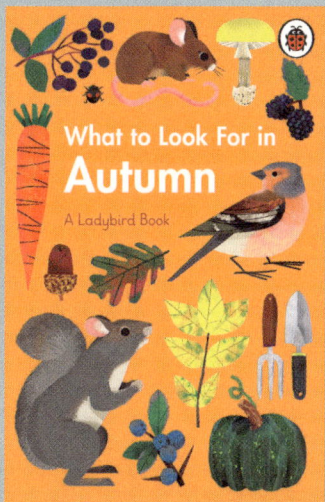

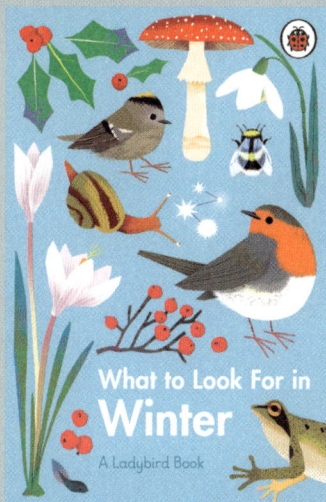

What to Look For in Autumn

9780241416167

What to Look For in Winter

9780241416228

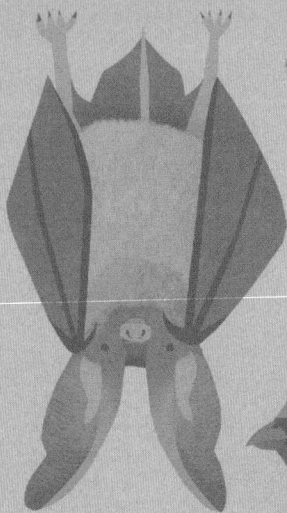

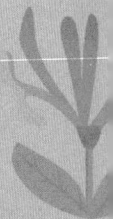

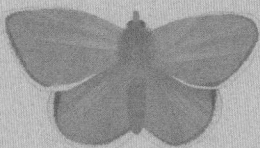